JESUS
AND THE
KINGMAKERS

Harrison House Books
by Joseph Z

JESUS
AND THE
KINGMAKERS

JOSEPH Z

Published by Harrison House Publishers
Shippensburg, PA 17257

ISBN 13 TP: 978-1-6675-0959-4
ISBN 13 eBook: 978-1-6675-0960-0

For Worldwide Distribution, Printed in the U.S.A.
1 2 3 4 5 6 7 8 / 28 27 26 25 24

CONTENTS

INTRODUCTION

I was inspired to write this book as a source of hope and inspiration, drawing directly from the scriptures and historical scenarios. My desire is to clarify the story of the magi who visited Jesus after His birth.

Most people know the famous song, "We Three Kings." This song is played every Christmas season. The understanding that only three wise men visited Jesus after His birth has become popular primarily because of this popular song. The basis of this understanding comes from the three gifts mentioned in Scripture. Matthew 2:11 says, "And when they had come into the house, they saw the young Child with Mary His mother, and fell down and worshiped Him. And when they had opened their treasures, they presented gifts to Him: gold, frankincense, and myrrh." This scripture has been used to justify the story of three wise men.

I want to take you on a journey to discover the truth behind the magi, including where they came from and their origin. The history of the magi is so essential. Every detail in Scripture has a purpose. Taking things at face value can sometimes hinder or take away from how incredible something is. Going behind the scenes and examining the steps that took place years before Jesus' birth, all the way back to the book of Daniel, will help you understand the awe-inspiring historical context of the magi's visit and why they brought precious gifts to Jesus.

CHAPTER ONE

JESUS AND THE WISE MEN

I want to explore something that is often overlooked or misunderstood. I'm pretty sure you're going to find this topic quite interesting. It begins with a question: If Jesus had real physical wealth on earth, where did it come from? We are going to answer that question.

Jesus was given gifts at birth. These gifts were fit for a king, and not just any king—the King of the world. Let's talk about the story of the wise men in Scripture. The wise men are recognized mainly by their depiction during the Christmas season. Much of what we know of them is an image formed by tradition, not an accurate historical representation.

ORIGIN OF THE WISE MEN

Matthew 2 tells us these wise men's story and connection to Jesus. Historically, the wise men were called *magoi* in Greek, or magi, which means "powerful or great one." They were known for magic and mystical arts. The name magi found its way into Persian culture, part of the Parthian dynasty under these magi's governance. The office of the magi was equivalent to our current parliamentary houses or branches of government.

KINGMAKERS

The Bible additionally describes them as astrologers. Ancient history's description of these men from the East emphasizes their ability to read the stars; however, they also had the authority to validate kings. These "kingmakers," magi, or wise men, were involved with far more than the image depicting three kings on camels in the desert.

In the Bible, these kingmakers were mystical individuals from the order of the Chaldeans. There were way more than three of them. When they came to a location, they would arrive with the authority of an army. In addition to being astrologers, they were labeled magicians and were highly influential in the culture. These wise men were influential, had extraordinary capabilities, and had commanding authority equivalent to the government's. They possessed power and prestige and were capable of nearly paramilitary actions.

From biblical and historical points of view, they were astrologers, kingmakers, government officials, and magicians. Modern-day history might label them "magicians" as they were shrouded in mysticism. They observed the sky, the stars, and other heavenly bodies. Their governmental influence would be similar to that of Merlin, the magician, or the country's wizard, who endorsed King Arthur in legend. Another similarity, you could say, would be the relationship between King Aragorn and Gandalf, the wizard in *Lord of the Rings*. Stories such as these transcend history.

STARGAZERS

Through their ability to read the stars, the magi knew the time and season when an event of historical significance was taking place. They could ascertain when a king would be born, not just any king, but the King of the world. These kingmakers came from a far country looking for baby Jesus with a star leading their way. In Matthew 2, we learn that they came from the East of Judea. This eastern location refers to the Persian Empire.

THE SILK ROAD

Today, the Persian Empire is known as Iran and was formerly part of the Parthian Dynasty. This empire controlled the ancient Silk Route, or the Silk Road. Today, we live in a civilized world where we can instantly connect with anyone through a global communication network. In those early days, travel systems and trade routes were the only form of communication. The Silk Road was a marvel in its time, connecting everyone who had access to it and the rest of the world. They traded everything, including precious metals, gems, rugs, spices, silks, incense, and many other commodities.

One of the things about the Silk Road is that it is mainly responsible for the beginning of modern history. Its network of roads started small and, over time, began to traverse the entire ancient world. It connected everyone inland to civilizations on the coast. The Silk Road changed the world by connecting everyone. Some precious things hauled on the Silk Road's commercial landscape were gold, frankincense, and myrrh. These were some of the most valuable items the world trade could offer, and those who traded them were held in high esteem.

DANIEL'S INFLUENCE

The story of Daniel brings more clarity to the story of the magi and Jesus. The life of Daniel, as described in Daniel 1:20, reads, "And in all matters of wisdom and understanding about which the king examined them, he found them ten times better than all the magicians and astrologers who were in all his realm." This passage talks about Daniel and his three comrades. It says they were ten times better than all the magicians and astrologers in their realm.

The magicians and astrologers mentioned in that passage were Chaldeans. If you look critically at it, you'll see that the wise men searching for Jesus were descendants of the Chaldeans in Daniel 1. These Chaldeans studied the stars and mystical arts, yet the Bible tells us that Daniel was ten times better than them and was

7

eventually given charge because of his excellent spirit. Daniel oversaw the magicians and astrologers in Babylon and other places, including Persia. Daniel's influence over these individuals reset their course, and by reading the stars, they looked to a future day when something big was to come.

ZODIAC AND THE GOSPEL

If you've ever studied the stars, you'd know there's something called the zodiac. The zodiac is a counterfeit of something God initially put into order. If you study the zodiac, you will come across God's story. *History* is simply HIS-story. God's plan for star charts was to learn History through a biblical lens, not some mystical demonic lens. God wrote His covenants in the heavens and the story of Jesus in the stars. Sadly, mystical groups usurped the true purpose of studying the stars. They perverted the meaning of something that God put in the heavens for humanity to see—His handiwork.

The prophet Daniel came into the country and was made to oversee the ancestors of these Chaldeans. Under his authority, they transitioned from primarily magicians to the level of government officials. Even kingmakers, who fulfilled a similar role to what prophets are supposed to do, could anoint or declare a person a king. Kingmakers also had astrological knowledge.

THE MAGI TROUBLED HEROD AND THE CITY

Matthew 2:1-2 says, "Now after Jesus was born in Bethlehem of Judea in the days of Herod the king, behold, wise men from the East came to Jerusalem,[2] saying, 'Where is He who has been born King of the Jews? For we have seen His star in the East and have come to worship Him.'" Again, these are wise men or astrologers from the order of the Chaldeans. Because they were now under Daniel's influence, they came searching for the Messiah. They came looking for the King of the world.

Matthew 2:3 says, "When Herod the king heard this, he was troubled, and all Jerusalem with him." In other words, he was greatly disturbed or terrified. The magi's presence troubled Herod and all of Jerusalem. Why was their message such a big deal to these people? It is because they knew the magi's history and reputation of being kingmakers. This understanding terrified Herod. He must have asked them, "Are you here for peace or to put the city in a siege?" He must have also inquired if they came bearing a message or came to inform him that he was no longer king.

There must be a significant reason for the magi to come because these guys did not travel from a far country to Jerusalem for nothing. They didn't just show up as three people on a camel! I believe they came in like an army on a mission. They came bearing gifts for a king, which gave them away. Their coming made Herod and the whole of Jerusalem know that a new king was about to be anointed. They knew this because the magi came in "kingmaker mode." If three guys showed up in town, I don't think it would shake up the city or scare them. However, the case would be different if a well-known army came into town and their logo was recognized. Then, without needing an introduction, the people would quickly realize what their purpose for coming was.

They might easily conclude that this "army" came to do something serious—like anoint a new king.

CHAPTER TWO

WORSHIP THE KING

The magi had traveled 750 kilometers, or 466 miles, from the Persian Empire to Roman territory. Accompanied by an army of elite forces, these magi were without fear while passing through Roman territory. They arrived to ask Herod where the King of the Jews was because they were there to worship the Messiah. Herod saw these men with their army and considered their question a major threat to his reign as king. He knew at that moment that he had a contender for the throne, which had been given to him by Caesar Augustus. These magi were not afraid of anything; they were the most elite special force in the world and a force to be reckoned with.

The entourage that came with them had a history in Rome. When you study history, you realize these guys already had run-ins with Rome. Some commentators even suggest that the magi had temporarily removed Herod from office before and reinstated him.

The people of Jerusalem probably felt like citizens in the movie *Independence Day*, when in the film, they woke up to 15-mile-wide alien saucers over their significant cities and were highly terrified. They knew who this military entourage was; it possibly numbered in hundreds or thousands. I discovered something important about their visitation—the gifts they brought were part of what shook Herod and the whole of Jerusalem at large. Let's talk about these items they brought for the Messiah.

Befitting Gifts for the King

Typically, the king's culture demands that when kingmakers visit a new king, they don't just go to worship him. They also must come bearing gifts. I want to emphasize something before we proceed. I told you about the ancient world's Silk Road trade system and the precious commodities they traded. As a rational person, what kind of gifts do you think they would bring to honor and anoint a king they believed was the King of the world? Bear in mind, they aimed to impress and stand out like real kingmakers who came to anoint the greatest king they've ever heard of or met. Think about it—do you think they would travel that far from home, pass through military zones with their awestruck army, to present a substandard gift to the King of the world? I don't think so.

Remember, we said the most valuable commodities on the Silk Road were gold, frankincense, and myrrh. The Bible tells us this was precisely what the magi, led by a star, brought to the Christ Child. Jesus was given gifts beyond comprehension. Do you realize these gifts were given to Jesus and not His parents? Yes, that was the case. Jesus entered this world rich. It means He probably had more money than everyone in that region because of the gifts He received as a child. These gifts presented to Jesus became His royal property as a king.

GIFTS EQUAL TO THE RECIPIENT

The wise men brought gifts equal to the recipient. Jesus is the King, Lord, and Ruler over the world; they could see it through the prophecies of Daniel and the reading of the stars. When you recognize how significant this is, you realize that these astronomers, jurors, and biblical people knew that the King of the world was coming. They prepared gifts that were equal to His kingship. This behavior shows how great Jesus was in their sight. This point is crucial because it helps us understand that Jesus had everything in heaven and here on earth. These gifts were massive, yet He poured them out for us and laid them down for you. He became poor so you could be rich.

SOLOMON'S WEALTH

I want to drive home a point about Jesus and His wealth. All the kings in the Bible were just minor men, including Solomon. The Word of God says Solomon was the wealthiest man who ever lived. His story is kind of like an allegory; it's exciting. Solomon was the wealthiest man who lived, but did you realize that David took the land, paid for everything, and made Solomon wealthy? Solomon inherited his father's throne. You could shadow this to Jesus inheriting the earth.

Let's talk about Solomon for a minute. The Bible says that there was none wealthier than him. He had so much wealth during his reign that the streets had gold and silver strewn on them. This must have been overwhelming for the community. Think of it—silver and gold lying around like rocks. Kings also brought gifts to Solomon, who was just a mere human king, yet he basked in the glory of his opulent wealth. Solomon's experience was luxuriant and over-the-top extravagant. He possessed an overwhelming amount of wealth.

I want you to pay close attention to Matthew 12:42, which says, "The queen of the South will rise up in the judgment with this generation and condemn it, for she came from the ends of the earth to hear the wisdom of Solomon...." Solomon was the wealthiest man ever. He was loaded with lots of stuff, including wisdom. But without a doubt, his understanding was without comparison. Solomon's greatness was in his wisdom and wealth.

GREATER THAN SOLOMON

The queen of the south shall rise up in the judgment with this generation, and shall condemn it: for she came

*from the uttermost parts of the earth to hear the wisdom
of Solomon; and, behold, a greater than Solomon is here.*

—Matthew 12:42 KJV

Yet, wonderfully, we have someone greater than Solomon available for us. If we consider the scenario in the Garden of Gethsemane in Matthew 26:47-55, Jesus could have decided to exercise His power by resisting arrest. He could have said, "You can't do anything to Me because I'm the reason you're alive." Instead, He said, "You're allowed to put Me in shackles and take Me into captivity, because it's been given to you to do so. However, you should know that I could at any moment call on more than twelve legions of angels to come down and destroy the earth." If you've ever studied that, you know that He could have destroyed the world several times over by saying, "God, I refuse to do it. I don't want to die on the cross."

We must understand that Jesus had all of heaven at His fingertips, just like He had all the earth, and at birth, He received an unbelievable amount of wealth. I believe He never accessed this wealth to the level He could have. Neither did He access all of heaven's armies when He was going to be crucified. Remember, Jesus, who was materially

and supernaturally rich, became poor for your sake. Why?
So that through Him, you can have access to that supernatural ability. You can also access natural wealth through Him
because He paid a gruesome price to give you this access.

THE STAR

There has been a lot of controversy over the star. Some
people have said it was the North Star, while others
believe it was an angel. Others talk about it being Planet
X. These magi studied the stars like sailors study the sky,
which led to using compasses to navigate the sea. They
rejoiced when the magi finally identified the star they
were looking for.

The truth is, we don't know exactly what the star was.
It appeared along the way and over the house where Jesus
was. God could have illuminated one star above the others
to serve as a GPS for them. He is the same God who sent
fire to burn Elijah's sacrifice; thus, anything is possible with
Him. What makes this whole narrative regarding the star
fascinating is that the magi, experts in their field, could read
the stars. So often, we overcomplicate the simple things that

are right in front of us. These guys were astrologers; it was their job to read the sky. The addition of this unknown, supernatural shining star must have thrilled them!

Again, there is precedent for these types of miracles. A pillar of fire led Moses and the children of Israel by night and a cloud by day; fire came from the heavens to burn Elijah's sacrifice. Yes, all these things happened. Nonetheless, what was the star? Where was the star? Can we still find the star today? Maybe you can, but this likely was a supernatural manifestation guiding them. As astrologers, they knew how to read the sky and had prophecies concerning the coming of the King of the world, given by Daniel. The prophet Daniel would have trained the forefathers of these wise men and mentored them in the practice of reading the heavens without involving diabolism. According to the Scripture, they followed their charts, and upon the miracle of the star appearing, they found exactly where Jesus was laid.

When they saw the star, they rejoiced with exceedingly great joy.

—Matthew 2:10

When the Bible says, "they rejoiced with exceedingly great joy," it means they began to go wild with excitement! All the military convoy, along with the magi, began to shout and jump up and down at the appearance of this star. We can only imagine the volume and power of this entire group of remarkable people shouting in the desert. It would be like a Superbowl score-winning moment.

Chapter Three

DELIVERY OF A FORTUNE

There was an allusion to the magi's gift of great wealth in Psalm 72. I believe these wise men or Chaldeans knew they were fulfilling Psalm 72:1-10. Psalm 72:10-13 says, "The kings of Tarshish and of the isles will bring presents; the kings of Sheba and Seba will offer gifts." These verses contain the prophecy of Jesus being presented with precious gifts. "Yes, all kings shall fall down before Him; all nations shall serve Him." This is a prophecy of the magi coming to worship Jesus. "For He will deliver the needy when he cries, the poor also, and him who has no helper. He will spare the poor and needy, and will save the souls of the needy." This scripture makes two references to the poor and needy, which I find fascinating; one says He will spare the poor.

Isaiah 61:1 says that Jesus preaches the gospel to the poor, and the gospel means good news. What is good news to the poor? It's not just salvation but also the realization that you no longer have to be poor. The good news for poor people is that they no longer have to be poor. That scripture also mentions the needy. It says that He will save the souls of the needy. He spares the poor by saying you should not be poor anymore, and then He begins to save the souls of the needy.

Earlier, we discussed how Herod and the whole of Israel were terrified; Isaiah 60:6 paints a picture of this scenario. It says, "The multitude of camels shall cover your land." People used a multitude of camels in those days to carry loads while traveling. In our context, they brought gold, frankincense, and myrrh to Jesus, which is in accordance with the scripture that continues in verse 6, "The dromedaries and Midian and Ephah; all those from Sheba shall come; they shall bring gold and incense, and they shall proclaim the praises of the Lord." They followed a star or star chart in search of Jesus, and when they got to Jerusalem, the Bible says a multitude of camels covered the land.

You can see why Herod was afraid—not only were these kingmakers in town, whom he had already had

encounters with, but they brought an enormous and unbelievable amount of wealth. The treasure they carried under
military protection was vast. The sheer amount of person-
nel and soldiers could have ranged into the thousands. You
can see why the people of Israel, or children of Jerusalem,
were terrified or troubled. If the camels covered the land,
many of them carried gold, frankincense, and myrrh, not
to mention a variety of other items customary to bring to
even a low-level king.

> *When they had heard the king, they departed; and, lo, the
> star, which they saw in the east, went before them, till it
> came and stood over where the young child was.*
>
> —Matthew 2:9 KJV

When the magi came to see Jesus, He was no longer in
Bethlehem. He was now two years old and in a house in
Nazareth. Joseph, Mary, and Jesus were only in Bethlehem
for 40 days. From there, they traveled to Nazareth.

> *When they saw the star, they rejoiced with exceeding
> great joy. [11] And when they were come into the house, they
> saw the young child with Mary his mother, and fell down,
> and worshipped him: and when they had opened their*

treasures, they presented unto him gifts; gold, and frankin-
cense and myrrh. [12] *And being warned of God in a dream*
that they should not return to Herod, they departed into
their own country another way.

—Matthew 2:10-12 KJV

A LITERAL FORTUNE WAS DELIVERED

Matthew 2:11 says, "And when they had come into the house, they saw the young Child with Mary His mother, and fell down and worshiped Him. And when they had opened their treasures, they presented gifts to Him: gold, frankincense, and myrrh." Note the plural word *treasures*. These guys gave Jesus a lot of treasures consisting of very precious items. This passage says that the magi presented *gifts*, another plural word. These were royal gifts. The magi's cargo included treasures beyond gold, frankincense, and myrrh.

As they "opened their treasures," the meaning of this goes far beyond a hand-sized box. Opening their treasures means to clear a way because they were carrying an enormous number of gifts into the house. History has left us with much documentation, and researchers have gathered data to know precisely what the Persians and magi would have brought.

In this Eastern culture, diplomatic gifts were in proportion to the size of the recipient. These magi knew they were bringing treasure to the King of the world. It would have been insulting to the king if they did anything less than the most magnificent treasure available. How much more to the King of the world! It was customary to give even low-level kings gifts such as vases, lamps, plates, dishes, carpets, rugs, urns, regal clothing, and various exotic materials. The catalog of gifts would have amounted to an absolute fortune.

Diplomatically, if you were going to see a king at birth or any point, you would bring your very best gift even if you were not royalty yourself. Some Bible scholars believe that the offering of gold and precious spices suggests that the magi, who had given these gifts, were wealthy, as the items themselves were of great value.

First, the gold, frankincense, and myrrh were of great value. Second, it's just like how Jesus died on the cross. Some people don't see the fact that He died and was resurrected on the third day as being a huge deal.

The type of gold they brought was the highest quality reserved for dignitaries, ambassadors, and heads of state. Frankincense was difficult to make and costly to transport due to its distance from the area. It was known as the favorite fragrance of kings. Myrrh was an ointment to embalm the dead. This would be a strange gift to give a two-year-old king, but this gift prophetically spoke of Jesus' death.

Frankincense and myrrh alone were worth more than gold. These magi pulled out all the stops; after all, they gave to the King of the world! The estimated cumulative value of all the gifts Jesus was given is staggering. For a low-level king, 110 kilos of gold were the standard gift; converting it into today's value, some estimate it would be valued at more than $5 million. This is the lowest level a king would receive. It can be speculated that Jesus' fortune was the most any king had ever received from these kingmakers. Some speculate it was likely upward of a billion dollars in today's value—possibly far more!

When you get this concept, you begin to understand that the magi were not just three kings riding along on donkeys, camels, horses, or whatever medium of transportation they employed because it wouldn't have been safe for them. The road could have been filled with thieves who could have robbed them because of the gifts they carried. They were Chaldean and astrologers who were under Daniel's tutelage. I believe that with Daniel's help, they were able to interpret the scripture. When they coupled this knowledge with their astrological skills, they were able to see the coming of the King of the world, which was the coming of Jesus, the Messiah. They felt a sense of shared responsibility to bring gifts to the King. When they came, their presence terrified Herod and the entire city, but they went further and sought the Lord God Almighty and found Him. When they did, I believe they fell and worshiped Him.

Please note that they didn't just present these gifts for the sake of it. Neither did they give them to Mary and Joseph, his parents; these gifts were meant for King Jesus. Since Jesus Himself was the recipient of these gifts, only He could be the one to give them away. This was an inheritance given to the firstborn Son of God. A firstborn child carries a significant meaning. In the book of Deuteronomy 21, we learn that the firstborn gets everything or a double portion of what the parents leave behind. Only that firstborn child had the authority to receive such a gift and give it away.

The point is that the magi gave these gifts to Jesus, but Mary and Joseph had to be responsible for them because Jesus was a child. Realizing the extreme lengths God went through to get Jesus provision for His life on earth is a profound reality.

JESUS' GIFT TO THE WORLD

Oh, the depth, the height, the breadth, and the width of God's love. How measureless is the love of God for you! Jesus did this because He knows you can't worship with what you don't have. You can't sacrifice something you don't have. You can't give away or deny something you cannot access. Thus, Jesus became poor when the day came when He poured out the very wealth given to Him from birth.

Jesus received wealth as a child, yet He had no ability to spend it. His mother and father, Joseph the carpenter, had to serve as fiduciaries for Him.

CHAPTER FOUR

THE MAGI BROKE HELL'S ECONOMY OVER JESUS

These magi are a tremendous example of individuals who broke hell's economy in their generation. Armed with a prophecy and the means to honor the King of the world, these individuals traveled great distances only to be met with the manipulation of a tyrant (Herod). It takes a Word from God and the strength to rise against the scheming plots brought on by the kingdom of darkness, and that they did! Mission accomplished—they broke hell's economy by fulfilling their assignment of equipping Jesus with the God-ordained resources from the heavenly Father to His one and only Son.

These magi have a place in history as a vital part of the greatest story of man's redemption! It is fascinating to recognize that the Lord used these magicians and astronomers for such a profound task. These mystics were truth seekers, not unlike Cornelius, whose alms and gifts to the poor came up before the Lord, resulting in the salvation of his household (Acts 10). In every generation, there are those who may be mystics or truth seekers.

Generally, mystics are defined as those searching for truth through symbolic or spiritual interpretation. This can lead to occult and demonic practices; however, in a pure form, these are individuals like the magi searching for more than what the natural world has to offer.

They are some of those who are willing to accept the truth and believe in things that are outside of the box. These are the kind of people who say, "I just want to know what the truth is." These mystics were trying to honor God in all the light (knowledge) they had. It reminds me of the scripture where Jesus instructed His disciples not to forbid others from attempting to cast out demons. Jesus said about these people, "He that is not against us is for us."

And John answered and said, Master, we saw one casting out devils in thy name; and we forbade him, because he followeth not with us.[50] *And Jesus said unto him, Forbid him not: for he that is not against us is for us.*

—Luke 9:49-50 KJV

Their ancestors were under Daniel, and the knowledge of prophetic Scripture was learned during this period and traveled down through the magi's generation. This is the reason they came to worship the King of the world with gifts. You might ask, "How in the world would God work with these kinds of people?" I think Matthew 2:12 sort of answers this question. It says, "Then, being divinely warned in a dream that they should not return to Herod, they departed for their own country another way." Why did God speak to these magi? For the same reason we mentioned earlier regarding Cornelius, whom God spoke to through an angel. God is a "heart" God; He is not as religious as we have been led to believe.

God has spoken to many different types of people throughout history. Consider King Abimelech in Genesis 20. God warned him in a dream not to touch Abraham's wife, Sarah, and the king obeyed. Let's consider the people of Nineveh. God sent Jonah to preach to them, and they did not take offense at God's judgment but instead had contrite hearts. They earnestly wanted to know what they were doing wrong and how they could amend their ways.

In Matthew 2:12, God additionally spoke to the magi about Herod in their dreams. It is possible He spoke to all of them simultaneously in their dreams. This greatly suggests that these men were spiritually centered on the Lord.

The time of these events was the intertestamental period in history. In each generation, there are those who are called upon by the Lord to break the plans of the devil. Breaking hell's system is the plan of God through whoever will listen. His highest desire is that all mankind be saved, and He will provide supernatural provision to those who want to help Him in His mission to see the world saved.

When Jesus died at 33, if these wise men were still alive, they would have given their lives to Him. They would have made Him their Lord, accepted Him completely, repented of their sins, and became preachers of the gospel.

HEROD'S PLOT

Herod must have plotted something evil against the magi while he awaited their return. Somehow, even though these guys were a force to be reckoned with, there was probably a lot of trouble in the city during their absence. Their presence in Jerusalem must've caused quite a stir, and I speculate Herod would have manipulated the situation in his favor. The Lord warned them, in essence saying, "Don't go back. You might get manipulated. Something could happen to you, or Herod could dig up a trail in your camp that might lead him to where Jesus is." The wise men went home another way and avoided Herod. They listened to God. Not only did God speak to them, but they listened to God's Voice.

We've talked about this in previous chapters—these mystics from afar knew the scriptures, which is a very powerful thing to realize. They were on a mission from God. I urge you, my friend, not to hold back; let the Master use you to do His purpose. If God will work through individuals such as these magi, He will certainly work through your life.

GOD WANTS TO USE YOUR LIFE MORE THAN YOU REALIZE

If the Lord would use those who did not know the salvation of Jesus, how much more would He use your life to rise and break off the powers of darkness from your generation? Do not say you are small, unable, weak, cannot speak, or offer any other excuse. God loves to take the unqualified and smash the evil plans of the qualified. He delights in using the foolish things of the world to shame the wise and in beating the odds through the humble. God is not religious; He loves you and is thrilled at the opportunity to shock the lives of many through you. Get ready to be a sign and a wonder to your generation by simply saying yes!

CHAPTER FIVE

ON A BAD DAY, YOU'RE THE BEST THERE IS!

It must be said, and you must hear it. In a world of darkness, in a culture gone rogue, creating a slope for evil to plunge deeper into its own mire—society will arrive at a place of chronic desperation. Surely God has a plan! Surely God has something prepared to spring on the world at the last moment! He must have a secret weapon; His very best, the last line of defense, the accumulation of generations who have paved the way in blood to where we are. The great God of heaven certainly must have His plan and response to launch against this onslaught of darkness!

He does!

It's you!

GOD BELIEVES IN YOU

You are marked and called by God to stand in the blood of Jesus and take territory unlike any other time in history. This is it! We are at the 12th hour; we are at the one-yard line, and He has chosen you to be alive during the most significant time in our history. No matter the cost, no matter the assaults, regardless of the global crises coming in wave after wave. Remember this—on a bad day, you are the best there is!

God is so smart, and He chose you to be present during this time. If you don't believe it, believe in the God who placed you on the planet. He believes in you and calls you to be the answer for this generation because Christ is in you, the hope of glory!

YOU'RE MADE IN HIS IMAGE AND LIKENESS

One of the greatest lies the devil told goes to the beginning when Satan spoke to Eve in the Garden. "For God knows that in the day you eat of it your eyes will be opened, and you will be like God…" (Genesis 3:5). The devil attempted to persuade God's original children into believing a half-truth regarding their relationship with the Father and their identity. The devil's intent was to convince Adam and Eve that God was holding back something from them. The actual truth was they were already like God! "God said, 'Let us make man in Our image, according to Our likeness…'" (Genesis 1:26). God's very first action toward mankind was to bless them. God's very first words were "be fruitful and multiply" (Genesis 1:28).

The devil's lies are the same lies today. He instills a sense that you don't deserve anything from God and that God is withholding something from you. This kind of thinking is a lie from hell! God's desire has always been that His kids occupy and take over the family business. God created it; He wants His family to run it all.

YOUR PRESENCE SHOULD DEMAND AN EXPLANATION

When walking in the midst of a dark and perverse generation, remember, you're different. The world is dead; you're alive. This means your presence should demand an explanation. Whenever you show up, Jesus just walked in, because He resides in you. It's your time for confidence—shake off the old grave clothes, be loosed of everything that so easily entangles you, and run with endurance the race that is set before you. Just like Jesus, the Author and Finisher of our faith, who for the joy set before Him endured the shame. You, my friend, were that joy set before Him!

IT'S ONLY FOREVER

A man of God named Dave Duell, whom I loved and ministered with, would often say, "Hey, it's only forever!" He graduated to heaven a few years ago. As I go through life and do everything possible to impact the world for Jesus, his words come back to me: "It's only forever." Knowing that you have an eternal destination is a comfort, but it also gives a sense of determination. Eternity is where we will receive the rewards or results of missed assignments. This personally gives me a drive to live for significance.

In eternity, you will not be floating on a cloud or in a nebulous state of consciousness, barely recognizing other saints who have gone before you. What we have to look forward to, even on the lowest level, is absolutely amazing. It is not an abstract experience; it's far more real than the "here and now." Eternity is a place of rewards and new assignments for the righteous.

KINGS AND PRIESTS

And has made us kings and priests to His God and Father, to Him be glory and dominion forever and ever. Amen.

—Revelation 1:6

And He has on His robe and on His thigh a name written: KING OF KINGS AND LORD OF LORDS.

—Revelation 19:16

Jesus is the King of kings and the Lord of lords. Understanding the meaning behind this is a wonderful and sobering thought. We are called to rule and reign forever with Jesus. We are kings and lords. He is the King of the kings and Lord of the lords!

And as they heard these things, he added and spake a parable, because he was nigh to Jerusalem, and because they thought that the kingdom of God should immediately appear.[12] He said therefore, A certain nobleman went into a far country to receive for himself a kingdom, and to return.[13] And he called his ten servants, and delivered them ten pounds, and said unto them, Occupy till I come.[14] But his citizens hated him, and sent a message after him, saying, We will not have this man to reign over us.[15] And it came to pass, that when he was returned, having received the kingdom, then he commanded these servants to be called unto him, to whom he had given the money, that he might know how much every man had gained by trading.[16] Then came the first, saying, Lord, thy pound hath gained ten pounds.[17] And he said unto him, Well, thou good servant: because thou hast been faithful in a very little, have thou authority over ten cities.[18] And the second came, saying, Lord, thy pound hath gained five pounds.[19] And he said likewise to him, Be thou also over five cities.[20] And another came, saying, Lord, behold, here is thy pound, which I have kept laid up in a napkin:[21] for I feared thee, because thou art an austere man:

*thou takest up that thou layedst not down, and reapest
that thou didst not sow.²² And he saith unto him, Out
of thine own mouth will I judge thee, thou wicked servant. Thou knewest that I was an austere man, taking
up that I laid not down, and reaping that I did not
sow:²³ wherefore then gavest not thou my money into
the bank, that at my coming I might have required mine
own with usury?²⁴ And he said unto them that stood by,
Take from him the pound, and give it to him that hath
ten pounds.²⁵ (And they said unto him, Lord, he hath
ten pounds.)²⁶ For I say unto you, That unto every one
which hath shall be given; and from him that hath not,
even that he hath shall be taken away from him.²⁷ But
those mine enemies, which would not that I should reign
over them, bring hither, and slay them before me.*

—Luke 19:11-27 KJV

*He who is faithful in what is least is faithful also in much;
and he who is unjust in what is least is unjust also in
much.¹¹ Therefore if you have not been faithful in the
unrighteous mammon, who will commit to your trust the
true riches?¹² And if you have not been faithful in what*

is another man's, who will give you what is your own?[13]
*No servant can serve two masters; for either he will hate
the one and love the other, or else he will be loyal to
the one and despise the other. You cannot serve God and
mammon.*

—Luke 16:10-13

REIGNING OVER TERRITORY IN ETERNITY

This parable in Luke 19, as well as Luke 16:11, has prophetic implications. Rewards for how stewardship is han-
dled here on earth will play out in eternity. Notice that
the types of rewards involve ruling over territory—cities,
to be exact. Please understand, you were not created to
live in heaven. Adam was created to rule the earth. In the
end, there will be a new heaven and a new earth. The new
earth is where we will reside and begin ruling. Much like
the Garden of Eden, man was told to tend to it and take
dominion over it. It is highly likely that had Adam not
fallen, he and Eve would have continued expanding the

Garden until the entire earth was under their dominion. It could be that they would have continued into the solar system until they even occupied other planets, causing them to flourish as well.

It's only speculation, but ruling and reigning with Jesus for eternity could mean we will be responsible for expanding God's kingdom to the ends of the universe. This might be how we would exercise our kingship and lordship. Who knows what He has in store for His sons and daughters after we get past this present age. The book of Revelation states that we will reign forever and ever.

> *And there shall be no more curse, but the throne of God and of the Lamb shall be in it, and His servants shall serve Him. ⁴ They shall see His face, and His name shall be on their foreheads. ⁵ There shall be no night there: They need no lamp nor light of the sun, for the Lord God gives them light. And they shall reign forever and ever.*
>
> —Revelation 22:3-5

What we do here and now is what will determine the level of reigning we will experience in eternity.

GOING RED

> *And they overcame him by the blood of the Lamb and by the word of their testimony, and they did not love their lives to the death.*
>
> —Revelation 12:11

Now is the time to stand up and enforce the covenant promises on this earth. You are called to rise in this time, overcoming by the blood of the Lamb and the word of your testimony, and not loving your life even unto death. This is the formula for overcoming. In reference to the blood of Jesus, His covenant, and all that it provides, we use the phrase "going red." For many years, our ministry and audience have become known as the "Red Church." Not a denomination, not a doctrine, just a simple understanding that anyone, anywhere, who is washed in the blood of Jesus will rise, regardless of doctrinal differences that are not heaven or hell issues.

If Jesus is your Lord and you're covered by His blood, then I consider you part of the Red Church. We are His blood-bought body. We know our covenant rights. "Going red" is a statement declaring Jesus is Lord, and we are covered in His blood. We're "going red" no matter what circumstances we face in our lives. This also carries the idea that we are to take the covenant of God to the ends of the earth by the preaching of the gospel. This is the highest responsibility a believer has. It is the number-one way we break hell's economy and make God rich. You need to "go red" and take the message of Jesus to everyone you meet.

This is what God gets behind financially and in every other resource and way that He has made available to us. He who wins souls is wise, according to Proverbs. Why? Because lost souls are the only thing God does not have. Going Red means we take the gospel of Jesus to them, winning them to Christ and making disciples. A person being saved is the only true thing we can give to God. A person saved and matured in the things of God is more valuable to the Lord than finding a gold mine. To Him, it would resemble receiving an inheritance of untold value. Psalm 116:15 gives us insight into the value God places on His mature saints.

Precious in the sight of the Lord is the death of His godly ones.

—Psalm 116:15 NASB

Precious (important and no light matter) in the sight of the Lord is the death of His saints (His loving ones).

—Psalm 116:15 AMPC

The word *precious* in this verse is the Hebrew word *yaqar*, which also means "costly." This verse could read: "Costly in the sight of the Lord is the death of His godly saints."

When God loses mature believers to the grave, although He is thrilled to receive them in eternity, the cost is great on earth. Why? Because of their experience and wisdom, the abilities they possessed from years of maturing their gifts and knowing Him at a high level, are no longer working on the earth. Within the global population, there are very few who know God through a disciplined life of surrender, prayer, and consecration. Few are tenured warriors, accurately tuned in to the Holy Spirit, having weaponized faith from years of practice. These rare ones are highly effective agents for the kingdom and are not easily replaced. The Lord of heaven only has so many of this caliber of believer in each generation.

Remember, there are two things that make God rich:

1. Lost souls getting saved. Converts who are transformed into mature believers through discipleship.
2. A tenured saint who lives a long life enforcing God's will on earth. These individuals are highly valuable to the Lord.

There are darker days coming than we ever imagined. The kind of darkness our society is facing must be met by supernatural, mature believers. If Jesus tarries, the body of Christ must step into its full potential as an unbeatable global superpower, highly capable of thwarting the powers of darkness. Together, we can effectively destroy the works of the devil; should the *catching away* of the saints happen sooner than later, the kingdom of darkness would breathe a sigh of relief!

A fire-baptized church, red with the blood of Jesus, releases a punishment against the darkness that it cannot tolerate. The current plans of evil cannot prevail with the church of Jesus Christ standing in the way.

Together we can break hell's economy, destroy strongholds over many lives, and ultimately change the world. It begins with you. You are the answer. My friend, I am so thankful you took this journey with me. I bless you in the name of Jesus and declare that your best days are before you and that you will discover your place in the body of Christ.

I hope to see you out there on the battlefield. As a united front, we will push back the agenda of darkness. I believe you will rise to your divine occasion. God believes in you, and so do I. Don't shrink back—you are so valuable to all of us. As you continue to give your yes to the Lord, He will position you.

For Jesus,

Joseph Z

ABOUT JOSEPH Z

Joseph Z is a Bible teacher, author, broadcaster, and international prophetic voice. Before the age of nine, he began encountering the Voice of God through dreams and visions. This resulted in a journey that has led him to dedicate his life to preaching the gospel and teaching the Bible, often followed by prophetic ministry.

For nearly three decades, Joseph planted churches, founded Bible schools, preached stadium events, and held schools of the prophets around the world. Joseph and his wife, Heather, ministered together for 15 years and made the decision in 2012 to start Z Ministries, a media and conference-based ministry. During this time, they traveled the United States, taking along with them a traveling studio team, live broadcasting from a new location several times a week.

A season came when Heather became very ill due to hereditary kidney failure. After three years of dialysis and several miracles, she received a miracle kidney transplant. Joseph and Heather decided to stop everything, they laid everything down and ministered to their family for nearly three years.

In 2017 Joseph had an encounter with the Lord and received the word to "go live every weekday morning"—Monday through Friday. What started with him, Heather, and a small group of viewers, has turned into a large and faithful online broadcast family. Today, his live broadcasts are reaching millions every month with the gospel and current events—which he has labeled "prophetic journalism." He additionally interviews some of the leading voices in the church, government, and the culture.

He and Heather have two adult children who faithfully work alongside them. Joseph's favorite saying when ending letters, books, or written articles is, "For Jesus." As, "For the testimony of Jesus is the spirit of prophecy" (Revelation 19:10).

Joseph spends his time with his family, writing books, broadcasting, and training others in the Word of God.

For Further Information

If you would like prayer or further
information about Joseph Z Ministries,
please call our offices at

(719) 257-8050 or visit **JosephZ.com/contact**

Visit JosephZ.com for additional materials.

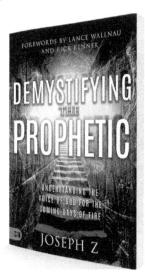

From

JOSEPH Z

Deploying God's Angelic Army

In the realm of the spirit, invisible forces contend over the will of God for your life, but you are not alone in this fight. Warrior angels—servants of fire—have been sent to minister to you as an heir of salvation.

Joseph Z, Bible teacher and prophetic seer, reveals the role of God's angelic warriors who carry out the Word of God on your behalf.

Servants of Fire delivers sound biblical instruction to unveil the realm of the spirit and bring to pass the will, plans, and purposes of God on the earth.

Understand how to partner with these servants of fire so you can experience the maximum impact of a victorious life in God!

Purchase your copy wherever books are sold

In the Right Hands, This Book Will Change Lives!

Most of the people who need this message will not be looking for this book. To change their lives, you need to **put a copy of this book in their hands.**

Our ministry is constantly seeking methods to find the people who need this anointed message to change their lives. **Will you help us reach these people?**

Extend this ministry by sowing three, five, ten, or *even more* books today and change people's lives for the better! Your generosity will be part of catalyzing the Great Awakening that many have been prophesying and praying for.

Made in the USA
Columbia, SC
19 December 2024

50000224R00037